CONTENTS

HOME BREWING .... ERROR! BOOKMARK NOT DEFINED.

CONTENTS 2

1 THE HISTORY OF HOME BREWING 5

    ALE... 5

    THE 1600'S 7

    ENGLISH VS. OTHER BEER 7

    THE 1800'S 8

    THE 1900'S AND PROHIBITION 8

2 REASONS FOR HOME BREWING 10

    BEER AND MONEY 10

    THE BEER CONNOISSEUR 11

    BEER AS FUEL 11

    SAVING MONEY 12

3 LEGALITY OF HOME BREWING 14

    STATE LAW 15

    BREWING VS. DISTILLING 16

4 ADVANTAGES AND DISADVANTAGES OF HOME BREWING 18

    HEALTH ADVANTAGES 19

    BRAGGING RIGHTS 19

    DISADVANTAGES 20

5 VARIETIES OF HOME BREWING 22
WINE BREWING 22
LIQUEURS AND CORDIALS 23
HOME BREW SODA POP 24

6 GLOSSARY OF HOME BREWING TERMS 26

7 ACCESSORIES NEEDED FOR HOME BREWING FROM SCRATCH 31
EQUIPMENT LIST 31

8 HOME BREWING KITS 35
BEER MAKING KITS 35
USING THE INTERNET FOR HELP 37

9 PROCESS OF HOME BREWING 38
AND FINALLY...GET BREWING! 38
PREPARING THE WORT 39
ADDING THE HOPS 39
CHILL THE WORT 39
PREPARING (PROOFING) THE YEAST 40
THE FERMENTER 40
ATTACH TUBING 40
MORE WAITING... 41
BOTTLING STEPS 41
TRANSFERRING BEER 42
BOTTLING THE BEER...FINALLY 42
CAPPING 42
YOU'RE DONE! 43
RECIPES 44

BARLEY WINE..44

OKTOBERFEST..44

10 THE FINISHED PRODUCT 46

HOME BREW FAQ 46

1
THE HISTORY OF HOME BREWING

The process of brewing beer has been around as an art for a millennium. It's only been recently, however, that practitioners have tried to turn it into an applied science.

The oldest American brewery is D.G. Yuengling & Son in Pottsville, Pennsylvania, which has been brewing beer since 1829. Although we think of home brewing and brewing of beer in general as starting in the 1800s, beer has actually been around for much longer than that. Home brewing and beer have always played a large and important part in our lives. In fact, it is believed that Noah provided for beer to be part of the provisions on the Ark!

ALE...

What we know today as beer was originally known as ale. Ale was made by fermenting the extract from grains and cereals. Certain herbs such as ground ivy and stinging nettle were used for flavoring and bittering. At the start of the 15th Century, people began to notice a difference between beer and ale, as beer was the hopped beverage that was made in Belgium. Beer and ale were the drink of the common people throughout the country before coffee, tea and cocoa were introduced. Monasteries were the location of some of the first commercial breweries in England.

Many families, specifically farmers, brewed their own ale (or beer), although there were professional brewers in town that made it as well. In fact, home brewing was a household industry in those days. Most of these professional brewers consisted of widows, because this was one of the few career choices open to widows. Workers at estates often received ale as wages. When taverns came into existence, they would each brew their own ale. They'd put a fresh bush outside of the place so those passing by would know there was fresh brew available.

THE 1600'S

In 1683, William Penn started a business of brewing beer in Pennsburg, to earn money as well as encourage people to drink beer instead of hard liquor, which seemed to cause bad tempers for many.

The early methods of brewing beer consisted of heating and soaking barley to encourage germination. The result of this mixture, called malt, was then mixed with water and brought to a boil until it formed the wort[1], which meant it was fermented. Hops[2] were then added to the boiling substance, to give it a distinctive aroma and pleasant yet bitter taste. Hops are used as a stability agent and for flavoring in beer. The liquid was then strained, at which time yeast was added. It was then allowed to ferment for a couple days.

ENGLISH VS. OTHER BEER

One major difference between brewing methods then and today is the timing process. Prior to the twentieth century, a rule of thumb or old time recipe determined the timing, as opposed to the modern equipment and technology used today. There was a difference between English beer and the early American beer.

When the English beer was made, they fermented it with yeast that floated on the top, whereas Germans used yeast that would stay on the bottom of the wort. When the Germans removed the yeast, they allowed the beer to

---

[1] Wort is the unfermented or fermented solution of malt used after the fermented mixture becomes beer

[2] Hops come from the Humulus plant, which bears female flowers in the shape of cones, which is what are used in the brewing process

age at low temperatures for weeks. This resulted in milder beer with a better aroma, making it a more popular style of beer. This beer took over the beer industry, so the floating yeast style of beer making was left for the making of ale. This was when the real distinction between beer and ale was made.

THE 1800'S

The late 1800's brought about many changes in the home brewing of beer. It became more difficult for the small businessperson or individual to compete with the larger breweries using up-to-date equipment. The addition of the railroad helped breweries distribute their beer around the nation. However, this made it a requirement that beer be able to withstand sitting for days, changes in temperature and getting shook up a lot of the time in transit. Chemical additives had to be removed, and pasteurization was necessary to prevent bacterial growth.

THE 1900'S AND PROHIBITION

Laws came into effect to make sure these requirements were followed. The early 1900s brought about the great Prohibition, a time when it was forbidden to sell any alcoholic beverages. This hurt the beer and liquor business drastically, but it did survive. After Prohibition was done, it took many years to get the people back in the habit of drinking beer rather than hard liquor, however.

Home brewing was made legal in 1976 and many small town craft brewers began making and marketing their own brands of beer, for sale to other businesses and areas. The sales of craft beer grew so high that they became competitive to some of the large brewers, who then began developing and marketing their own brands of beer.

Home brew is not near as popular as it once was, with the many different laws that have enacted through the years. Many have switched from the home brewing of beer to try their hands at wine and other liquors. The interesting thing about home brewing, however, is that with each beverage you make, you'll want to make more of some other variety just to experiment.

2
REASONS FOR HOME BREWING

People choose to home brew for different reasons. Some enjoy the art of making their own beer for personal consumption, while others home brew for the competitive spirit in amateur brewing contests. Others home brew to distribute it at social gatherings in their home, and some just do it for the hobby. Regardless of the reason, home brewing is still very popular and a lot of fun once you learn the art.

While the term "home brewing" may refer to the brewing of beer, alcoholic beverages and even some soft drinks, it's most often used when discussing the making of beer.

BEER AND MONEY

In the time of the Babylonians, beer was valued so highly that it was used as wages to be given to workers in lieu of money. Beer also played an important role to the Egyptians, as it was brewed for royalty, medical purposes and to be used in burials as a provision for the trip to the hereafter.

In the 1600s, when an Egyptian gentleman gave a lady a sip of his beer, it meant they were betrothed. Beer was also used for payment, trading, tithing and taxing in the medieval times. So, you can see whereas it's a form of refreshment today, beer was of much more importance in the past. As far back as the time 4,000 B.C., there were reasons for home brewing.

THE BEER CONNOISSEUR

If you've ever gone into a bar and observed beer drinkers, you'll see that some will order the cheapest beer in the bar or drink whatever brand the bar happens to serve. These are not true connoisseurs of beer.

A true and serious beer drinker has specific ideas of what they want in their beer. This is another reason why many choose home brewing. They like a specific style of beer and thrive to get just the right taste. Often there is a certain taste or style of beer that is not available commercially in their area, so they home brew to have access to it at any given moment.

Home brewing is, for many, not only convenient but a way to get the "live beer" taste. Almost all beer that is made is pasteurized, so you're not getting the natural taste. When beer is pasteurized, it has to be cooked, which takes out the carbonation. Commercial brewers "force carbonation" by taking the boiled off alcohol and mixing it with the pasteurized beer, which kills the yeast.

Without live yeast, the beer will not age properly, which affects the taste of the beer. Yeast not only improves the taste of beer, but the color and texture as well. The more beer ages, the better it tastes, which is a large reason why so many choose to home brew their own beer.

BEER AS FUEL

Another unique use for home brew is as a type of fuel. Many farmers that have a surplus of biomaterials such as rice, grains, potatoes, beets, etc. will use these materials to make their own alcohol to power their farm equipment. This is not only creative, innovative and energy efficient but also very economical. Cars and trucks can also use this cost-saving fuel as an alternative to paying the high prices at the pump.

SAVING MONEY

Home brewing beer can be much cheaper than purchasing equivalent type beers from commercial brewers, taverns or stores. Some home brewers choose to customize their recipes to their taste buds, which can cost more, but it's still usually more economical to home brew their own beer. Everyone enjoys a different taste to his or her beer. Not to mention, the great taste of freshly home brewed beer and the satisfaction of bragging to your friends that it's "your" beer.

Hop is the substance that gives beer the majority of its flavor and home brewing allows the maker to adjust the amount of hop flavor they put in their home brew.

Some devoted beer drinkers will adjust the amount of hop flavoring to be much higher than what they'd taste in a commercial beer. Home brewing also gives the person the opportunity to adjust the amount of alcohol that goes into the beer since some like high alcohol content whereas others like a milder beer flavor. Home brewers often like to experiment with darker or lighter beers and create some specialty beers that are unavailable on the open market or very rare and difficult to find.

Besides all the obvious reasons mentioned here for home brewing, it's just plain and simple a lot of fun. Once you get started, you won't want to quit. The anticipation of tasting your home brew is something that will keep you looking at the calendar. Your friends will probably all be on your doorstep on the "sampling day" when it's ready to drink.

3
LEGALITY OF HOME BREWING

Many people that are considering home brewing are concerned about the legality of this process. When we think of home brewing, Prohibition[3] comes to mind. This was a dismal period in the hearts of the many beer drinkers. It lasted far too long for their liking and took many years to get beer back on the market as strong as it was prior to Prohibition. The laws have changed a lot throughout the years, differently in many states and countries. Although home brewing is legal in most areas, you should check the legality in your state or country before you begin this fun process.

For many years after the Prohibition, home brewing was still illegal in certain areas of the United States in spite of the fact that Prohibition was repealed in 1933.

In 1978, in the U.S., an Act or bill was passed in Congress regarding home brewing during President Jimmy Carter's tenure in office. Many people mistakenly believe his bill allowed the home brewing of beer and wine, which was at that time still illegal. The bill that was actually passed made certain amounts of home brewed beer for personal use exempt from taxation. To further understand this bill and other bills regarding home brewing, you can check your local statutes.

---

[3] The time period from 1920-33 when the 18th Amendment restricted any alcoholic beverages to be manufactured, transported or sold anywhere in the United States

STATE LAW

The U.S. Constitutions have given each individual state the right to dictate the laws that will be in effect regarding the manufacture of home brewed beer or other alcoholic substances. Do not assume what is legal in one state will be legal in the next state. You don't want to see a new hobby of yours turn into a nightmare of legal issues.

Alabama, for one, clearly states that it is illegal in all counties to have any equipment or apparatus used to manufacture any kind of alcoholic beverages. It's also illegal there to have any illegally manufactured beverages brought into the state or transported inside the state.

Most of the states in the United States, however, do permit home brewing. There are some restrictions to the amounts of beer and the age of the person brewing. Most of these laws allow no more than 100 gallons of home brew per person per household and the person must be over the age of 21.

The maximum they can brew per year is 200 gallons. People that brew their own beers are restricted from selling it because the federal government taxes alcohol through excise taxes. Most Western countries have the same home brewing laws.

In Michigan, for instance, it's perfectly legal to brew your beer if you are over 21 years of age but only up to 100 gallons. You can give your home brew to other people, but you cannot sell it. The 100 gallons, incidentally, can be broken down into 20 5-gallon batches of brew. Many home brewers like making smaller amounts at one time so they can experiment with different flavors, colors and varieties.

Kentucky, on the other hand, prohibits anyone from having in their possession any apparatus used in the manufacture of any alcoholic beverage including home brew. While they are more concerned with illegal distilling, their laws can also be extended to the home brewing of beer.

BREWING VS. DISTILLING

Make sure that you don't confuse home brewing with distilling, which is *very* illegal in most states without certain permits and requirements. Again, it's very important for your peace of mind to check the specific laws in your locality to ensure that you won't be in legal jeopardy when you begin this hobby. Laws usually vary from country to country or state to state.

Sweden, for instance, allows you to home brew beer as long as you don't try to sell it and as long as you only use it for personal use.

The United Kingdom does not allow individuals to distill *or* sell their home brew products; it's legal to home brew beer or other fermented beverages. Home brewers do not have a cap on how much they can make, either.

Australia allows individuals to home brew their own beverages. The only restriction is that they cannot use a still. If any individual does own a still, its size cannot be larger than 5 liters and it cannot be used for the distilling of alcohol. The only use they may have for a still is to still certain substances like water or essential oils.

New Zealand allows home brewing and distilling as of 1996, when the ban against this was lifted. Individuals cannot distill spirits for their own personal use here, but they cannot sell or supply any alcoholic beverages unless they have the appropriate and correct license to do so.

South Africa allows individuals to manufacture fermented beverages in their home without any limits on the amount. Interesting, though, is that they cannot distill or sell their beverages or give them to any of their staff. The reasoning behind the law regarding their staff is unclear unless it's a legal issue involving intoxication.

What you will find in most states or countries is that the art of home brewing beer, wine or any fermented beverage is not what is against the laws; rather it's the sale of these products that's restricted. In many states, home brewing is not considered in their laws because they are more concerned with the manufacture and sale of hard liquors.

Because home brew is not commercially manufactured and sold, it's often not included in the statutes and regulations, leaving a lot of "gray area" in the law. Check the laws where you live before your begin just to be on the safe side.

4
ADVANTAGES AND DISADVANTAGES OF HOME BREWING

As with any hobby, there are advantages and disadvantages. The same is true with the home brewing of beer. However, most people that choose to home brew their own beer or other beverages will tell you that the advantages far outweigh the disadvantages.

When thinking of the number one advantage to home brewing, what comes to mind is the thing that means the most to beer lovers: taste.

Drinking commercially brewed beer as opposed to home brewed beer is like eating food when you have a cold. The food just doesn't taste like it should. You're not getting the full flavor.

When you're drinking commercially brewed beer that has been canned, bottled, exposed to outside air and knocked around, it's not going to taste anywhere near as good as fresh beer. If you don't believe this, open up a bottle of beer from the store, sniff it, and then sniff your freshly brewed beer. You'll see there's no comparison. Suffice it to say, you may not want to ever go back to drinking store-bought beer. This is probably the main advantage to brewing your own beer at home.

HEALTH ADVANTAGES

Brewing your own beer gives you the advantage of a healthy beverage. You may be surprised to see beer being described as a "healthy" beverage, but it's healthy in the aspect that you know what's going into the beer and what's not. If you've ever looked at the ingredients on a bottle of beer or any beverage for that matter, you'll probably find that you don't recognize half the ingredients that are going into the product. Worse than that is the fact that you are consuming these unfamiliar ingredients.

By brewing your own beer, you're getting all-natural ingredients that are familiar to you. You're also not getting all the preservatives you get when you drink commercial beers, so you're getting a better quality, better tasting beer.

You'll be familiar with the malt, barley, hops or whatever other natural ingredients you put in your beer. In your quest for good home brewing recipes, you'll find there are many varieties you can try.

Regardless of which recipe you finally decide to stick with, you'll still know what goes in the beer. What you'll like also with making your own beer is that you can control the alcohol content that goes in the beer. You may like higher alcohol content while your wife enjoys a milder beer.

When you buy a six-pack of beer, you're forced to drink a certain alcohol content unless you want to buy another six-pack of lower or higher alcohol content. When you make your own brew, you can mix it up and make a variety to suit everyone.

BRAGGING RIGHTS

Let's not forget about the bragging rights. When you're done making your beer, you'll probably want to have a party or social gathering to show off your home brewing skills. It will give you a lot of pride to be able to say that you made it yourself. Your friends will be impressed with your culinary skills and want to learn all they can about home brewing.

Home brewed beer has a fresh, natural taste that you will never get with commercially brewed beer. Not only is it a natural and better tasting choice, but also it's also very cheap compared to what you'd pay in a supermarket or liquor store.

The ability to experiment with the recipe will continue to be a source of fun for you. You'll never get tired of trying different recipes and making different types of beer. Whether it's mild beer, high alcohol content, dark or light beer, you'll love experimenting until you find the perfect combination for your new favorite recipe and drink.

Another advantage to home brewing is that in addition to having a premium tasting beer, you'll also get it at an affordable cost. Once you have all you need for your beer-making venture, you'll be able to make beer for just a few pennies a beer. The cheapest type of commercial beer you buy is at least a dollar a bottle. You'll be amazed at how much beer you can brew with that same dollar. As cheaply as you can make this beer, it's a shame that you can't sell it!!

DISADVANTAGES

Now we'll get into the disadvantages of home brewing your own beer or beverages. As discussed earlier, there are not near as many disadvantages as there are advantages. Besides the mess you'll have, one disadvantage to making your own beer is the initial start-up costs.

If money and budget is a major concern for you, you may find it difficult to comfortably buy everything you need to make your own beer. You can typically expect to spend a few hundred dollars to get you started. The equipment you need will cost around $100 plus a large kettle, which may cost up to $50 or more.

Keeping in mind your store's prices for liquid and dry yeast, the entire list of ingredients to make a 5 gallon match can cost from $25 to $50. You'll also want to buy some sanitizers and bottles, which will cost from $10 to $20 for 24 bottles of 12-oz. size. The bottles, however, can be reused repeatedly with sufficient cleaning.

Although you may continue to use your kitchen equipment to save money, many people choose to purchase special equipment designed specifically for beer making. Although these costs may sound expensive for starting off, many of them are one-time costs. Not to mention, you'll get a lot of beer for the amount of money you've invested.

Another disadvantage of home brewing your own beer is that you'll love the taste so much you may find yourself drinking more than you used to and more than you should! Your neighbors may be over more often then normal as well just to get some of your great-tasting free (at least to them) beer!

Home brewing can also be very messy and time-consuming, especially until you fully get the hang of it. You may decide you want a special room for this process if you'll be doing it frequently.

5
VARIETIES OF HOME BREWING

While hearing the terms, 'home brew' makes us most often think of beer, we are definitely not limited to beer. Beer is usually the beverage that most people interested in home brewing begin with, mostly because it's the most popular. Another reason is that it's the fermented beverage that is most often consumed.

Home brewing of beer is a fun experience for everyone, but especially individuals that enjoy a good beer as well as variety of different flavors. You can easily switch from a mild light beer to a dark beer with high alcohol content. This is what most home brewers enjoy the most about making their own beer: the ability to experiment until they find just the perfect taste.

WINE BREWING

If you're an individual that likes a good glass of wine, you'll love the opportunity of home brewing your own wine as well. For special occasions like social gatherings or formal affairs, many enjoy drinking hard liquor. Liquor is also a beverage you'll find fun and interested to make yourself.

Many wine brewing starter kits are available if brewing wine is what you want to try next. You won't be limited in your selection, as you'll be able to make red wines, white wines, port ice wine, champagne, hard cider and more.

Many of the companies that sell winemaking kit will help you with almost any kind of wine you choose to make. You tell them the flavor or type you want to make and they'll help you get the right winemaking ingredient kit.

If you're planning to make wine in the future, you may want to start saving your old wine bottles so you won't have to invest the money in new bottles. Some times the price of the new empty bottles can cost almost as much as the brew itself! Your initial investment will include the ingredients and equipment, which will run around $150. Much of the equipment that you've used for home brewing beer can be used for wine and other spirits. This is especially true if you've invested in higher quality equipment.

One thing that many home brewers enjoy about making their own wine is the flavor of the beverage while they're actually making it. The taste is usually so good that they find themselves drinking it while they're making it!

Another positive about wine making is that as easy as beer making is, most state making wine is even easier. The average batch size you'll get with the starter winemaking kits is 6 gallons. While that may not sound like a lot, it can go a long ways. It takes most people quite a while to go through even one gallon of wine, much less six unless they drink a lot. Most wine is not consumed as often or in such large quantities as beer.

A good rule of thumb with making wine is that the longer it sits, the better it's going to taste. If you find that it doesn't taste all that great, it's probably not ready. When it is ready to drink, you'll find that it's probably the best tasting wine you've ever had. The mixing and sanitation process for wine only takes about a half an hour with the bottling taking 1 to 2 hours. Then you wait six or more weeks to get great tasting wine. If the wine was made right with proper sanitation techniques, it will stay fresh for over a year. The use of premium corks and higher alcohol content will keep it fresh even longer.

LIQUEURS AND CORDIALS

In years past, the younger generation of drinkers was mostly beer drinkers. While they still enjoy a good beer today, they also love the taste of liqueurs and cordials. If you think it's mostly the older generation that enjoys these fancy drinks, you couldn't be more wrong. Everyone enjoys a good drink occasionally. This is the perfect way to increase the inventory in your home bar without spending an arm and a leg. The varieties of liquor that you can make are unbelievable.

Imagine the fun you'll have making Crème de Menthe, Crème de Cocoa, Irish Crème, Hazelnut, Cherry Brandy, Amaretto, Blackberry Schnapps, Peach Schnapps or Kahlua.

Most home brew kits for liqueurs and spirits will offer you a "base recipe" to start with and directions on the different flavorings you want to use. The one thing home brewed liquor has in common is the taste. You'll find no comparison between the flavors of home brewed liqueur compared to commercially brewed liqueur.

HOME BREW SODA POP

While you're so busy making your beer or liquor, your kids won't mind all the time it takes when they learn how to make their own soda. This relatively simple process only takes about an hour or so. You and they will love the flavor of the homemade ginger ale, Sarsaparilla, cream soda, cherry soda, root beer, cola and more. This tradition of making soda goes way back and is as educational as it is fun.

Making homemade soda doesn't require a lot of equipment. You'll need a siphon hose, a stirring spoon, bucket, a kettle for boiling and some soda bottles. You'll also need to get some caps and a bottle capper. By the way, your kids will love using the bottle capper and capping their own bottles! These are available in any store that sells homebrew supplies.

The only real ingredients you'll need are flavoring packs, yeast packs, sugar and water. Yeast packs made for beverages works better than bread yeast and will give your soda a better taste. You'll find that making soda is fun, quick and gives you and your family a great-tasting beverage.

Making your own soda consists of nothing more than mixing the sugar and water, adding the flavoring, mixing in the yeast, and then siphoning it into the bottles. Once the bottles are full, you put the caps on them and let them sit for 2 weeks.

6
GLOSSARY OF HOME BREWING TERMS

If you're new to the process of home brew, you're going to be reading many words and terms that will be unfamiliar to you. While you don't need to know what they all mean, it will be helpful to have a general idea of what most of them mean.

Keep in mind that some of these terms may be used in larger breweries rather than in your home brewing process. While there are many other brewing terms, these are the most common ones you will hear in your home brewing.

- **Additives**
  These substances such as preservatives, enzymes or antioxidants may be added to your home brew to add to the shelf life or simplify the brewing process.

- **Adjunct**
  This is a fermentable material used to make a cheaper or lighter-bodied beer and is a substitute for the traditional grains.

- **Alcohol**
  This may refer to either ethyl alcohol or ethanol. When the yeast works with the sugar in the malt, you get a certain alcohol content, which makes it intoxicating. Others describe it as the result of fermentation.

- **Alcohol by weight**
  This means the amount of alcohol that's in your beer as a percentage of the volume of beer. If a bottle states it's 2.5% alcohol by weight, it means it has 2.5 grams of alcohol for every 100 centimeters of beer.

- **Ale**
  This is a type of beer resulting from the use of malted barley and the top-fermenting types of brewers yeast. Most ale you'll find will have hops in them, which balances out the flavor.

- **All-malt**
  This is a beer that is made from all barley malt and no adjuncts.

- **Alpha acids**
  These are the bittering compounds in hops, which are extracted when the hops is boiled with the wort. The higher the alpha acid content, the more bitter the taste will be.

- **Barley**
  This is a cereal grain, which once malted, is used as mash when brewing beer.

- **Barrel**
  This is a unit of measure used to store beer. In the U.S., a barrel is equal to 31.5 gallons and 36 imperial gallons in Britain.

- **Beer**
  This term refers to the beverages that are flavored from hops and contain alcohol from fermenting grain such as malt.

- **Body**
  Body describes the thickness and property of your beer, either full or thin bodied.

- **Bottle capper**
  This is a device used to put your crown caps on your bottles. They can be used for home brewed beer or soda.

- **Bottling Bucket**
  This bucket, made of food grade plastic, has a spigot on the bottom for your convenience. The priming sugar is put in these buckets prior to bottling so they're sometimes referred to as priming vessels.

- **Bottom-fermenting yeast**
  This is one of the two types of yeasts that are used in brewing. Also known as "lager yeast", it's best when used at low temperatures and produces a clean crisp taste because it ferments with more sugars.

- **Brew kettle**
  This is the vessel where the wort that comes from the mash is boiled with the hops.

- **Carbonation**
  This is the sparkle created by the fermentation and caused by carbon dioxide.

- **Carboy Brush**
  If you use a carboy, this brush is a necessity for cleaning. It's perfect for getting to the inside of the carboy, which you'll have to do to clean it thoroughly.

- **Conditioning tank**
  This is the tank where the beer is stored after the initial fermentation. This is where it matures and becomes carbonated from the secondary fermentation.

- **Dry-hopping**
  This is when you add more hops to the aging or fermenting beer to increase the aroma or character of the hop.

- **Glass Carboy**
  These glass containers, which are also called fermentors, are used to store the beer while it ferments. The most common size is 5 gallons, although they come in a variety of sizes.

- **Hops**
  This is the female cone of the hop plant, which is used as a stability and flavoring agent in beer and other beverages.

- **Hydrometer**
  This instrument is used to measure the weight of the liquid (fermented or unfermented) in relation to the volume of water.

- **Lager**
  This term is used to describe a style of beer.

- **Malt**
  This is a grain, usually barley, which is soaked in water to get it to a certain moisture level. It then is germinated and then roasted to be used in the making of beer. The amount of roasting determines how light or dark the beer will be. They are used as adjuncts.

- **Racking cane**
  This is hard plastic tubing used when you're transferring the beer from the fermenting kettle to the bottling bucket or kettle. It bends on one end with a cap on the other end, which lets liquid flow through with the littlest amount of sediment.

- **Sanitizer**
  This is a special type of cleaner needed to sanitize (not just clean) all your equipment so it is sterile and will not promote bacteria. Some people use unscented bleach for this.

- **Siphon hose**
  This hose is used to get the beer from the vessel or barrel into the bottles, where it will be stored.

- **Sparge Bags**
  These bags re used to steep the specialty grains or hops in the brewing kettle. You can get reusable or disposable ones. They are steeped like tea bags.

- **Tubing**
  You'll need both small tubing (3/8" or ½" inside diameter) and large tubing (1" inside diameter) for your home brewing. The small tubing is used to get the beer out of the fermenter and for bottling. This large tubing is used during the initial fermentation process. Both size tubing are made of heavy-duty plastic.

- **Vessel**
  This is the container where the beer will be kept during the fermentation period.

- **Wort**
  This term is used to describe the mixture of the boiled water and malt after the hops has been added and before it's fermented.

- **Wort chiller**
  This is used to quickly chill the boiling wort to help the yeast pitch much quicker, which helps prevent the risk of infection. It's not a necessity, but makes things go much quicker and smoother. Some choose to make their own with a tubing bender and copper tubing.

- **Yeast**
  This ingredient helps with the fermentation in your home brew. While some people may try to use bakers yeast, brewers yeast will work much better.

7
ACCESSORIES NEEDED FOR HOME BREWING FROM SCRATCH

Now that you've read so much about home brewing, you're probably all excited and ready to get going. Although your beer will need a couple weeks from the first day until it's ready to drink, the actual home brewing process only takes a couple hours. Your main concern is probably what equipment you'll need to start home brewing. A lot of this will depend on how serious you are about home brewing. There are a few different factors you may want to take into consideration. The two main factors are your seriousness about home brewing and your budget.

If you are very serious about getting into home brewing and think you'll be doing it a lot, then you'll probably want to purchase some good home brewing equipment. On the other hand, if you are trying this for the first time and aren't sure if you'll do it again, you're not going to want to spend a lot of money on new home brewing equipment. Some of the household equipment you already have in your kitchen may suffice.

You also need to keep your budget in mind. If finances are a concern, you'll want to use what you already have in your kitchen or get your equipment as cheaply as possible. Many of the equipment pieces listed will make your home brewing easier, but aren't a necessity. One last thing you should consider when deciding what to buy and what not to buy is the amount of room in your home. Do you have extra space for additional equipment such as what you'll need for home brewing? Although many of the pieces are small, some of them are larger and will take up some space.

EQUIPMENT LIST

Here is a list of what you will need for beer making in your home.

- **A large pot**
  You'll need it to be at least 5 gallons (some use up to a 16-gallon size). The larger the better because there will be less chance for spills. This is usually a large stainless steel pot, sometimes called your brew kettle.

- **Tubing & Clamps**
  Clamps you can get at a store that sells home brewing equipment. Tubing is for the siphoning of the beer. You'll want food grade plastic tubing in both 3/8" inside diameter and 1" inside diameter. The large tubing is used during the initial fermentation period and the smaller tubing is used to get the beer from the fermenter for bottling.

- **Airtight Fermenter**
  You can purchase a glass carboy or use a 5-gallon size plastic bucket. This is where you will keep your beer while it's fermenting. Glass carboys come in different sizes although the most common size is 5 gallons. If it's in your budget, you'll want to go with the glass carboy because you won't have to worry about it leaking and it's very easy to clean if you have a large brush.

- **Carboy Brush**
  If you have invested in a carboy, you'll want to have a carboy brush, as nothing will clean it better.

- **Airlock and Stopper**
  There are different sizes of rubber stoppers, but you'll need 1 3/16" – 1 8/16" to fit a 5-gallon carboy. The stoppers go in the opening on the carboy and the air locks go in the stoppers. You can get a type 1 or type 2 air lock. They both work about the same, but the type 1 is easier to clean.

- **Bottle Filler**
  This will be used when you're bottling your beer and should be sized so it fits your other tubing. This is available where they sell homebrew supplies.

- **Thermometer**
  You'll need one that ranges from for 32°-220° F or 0°-100°C.

- **Hydrometer**
  This is not a necessity but is very handy. It comes with a sampling tube that will measure the beer's gravity before and after fermentation. This will let you know how much sugar has been converted to alcohol.

- **Bottles**
  You'll want to get returnable grade bottles because of the heavy duty cleaning they'll need, which they are strong enough to withstand. If you're brewing 5 gallons of beer, you'll need about 60 bottles if they're 12 oz and 32 bottles if they're 22 oz. Do not get the twist off cap bottles, but rather the ones where you pry off the lid.

- **Bottlebrush**
  While this is not a necessity, it will make washing your bottles a lot easier.

- **Bottle washer**
  This attaches to your faucet, goes inside the bottle, and sprays water all over the inside of the bottle, making cleaning easier.

- **Bottle caps**
  You'll need around 50 caps for 5 gallons of brew, which can be purchased at a homebrew supply store.

- **Bottle Capper**
  This handy little device can be held with both hands or there's also one that mounts to your table and only requires one hand.

- **Sterilizing solution**
  This is a necessity to keep your equipment sterile to prevent bacteria and risk of infection. Some people use unscented household bleach.

- **Funnel**
  You'll need this when you pour your beer from the pot (brew kettle) into the carboy.

- **Sparge Bag**
  These are used when you steep the specialty grains or hops in the brewing pot. They come in reusable nylon or disposable bags.

- **Racking Cane**
  This hard plastic tubing is used to transfer the beer from the fermenter to the bottling bucket. It has a bend on end and a special cap to allow the beer to flow through on the other end. It helps to minimize the amount of sediment that flows through.

- **Bottling Tube**
  This hard plastic tube has a spring-loaded tip that lets beer flow when it's pressed on the bottom of the beer bottle.

- **Bottling Bucket**
  This is made of food grade plastic and has a spigot on the bottom for your convenience. The priming sugars are put in these before bottling, which is why they're sometimes called priming vessels.

- **Wort Chiller**
  You don't have to have these, but they'll make the wort cool down a lot faster. They come in different sizes and styles. Many people make their own with a tubing bender and copper tubing.

8
HOME BREWING KITS

Now that you've read the list of all the possible home brew supplies you may need to get you started, you're probably wondering where to begin. Unless money is not a concern, you're not going to want to rush out and buy all the new supplies listed in Chapter 7.

The amount you choose to start with is a matter of personal choice. You can purchase everything on the list, but if you find home brewing is not something you're going to stay with, you'll have invested a lot of money for nothing. There are other ways to get start with your equipments without spending so much money. One of your options is purchasing a home brewing kit.

BEER MAKING KITS

You'll find many different brands of beer making kits on the market. The prices can range as low as $20 or as high as $200 and more. If you're just starting with the home brewing hobby, a home brewing kit is going to be the least expensive option. You may not have all the supplies you'd have if you purchased them all individually, but you'll have enough to get you started. You can always expand your inventory later.

A real popular beer making kit, The Beer Machine, can be yours for under $100 and has everything you need to start making beer. This at-home mini brewery is made with a sturdy design and construction complete with a custom pressure gauge that tells you carbonation level, brew quality and dispensing pressure. You'll have great tasting, high-quality beer in 7 to 10 days. The self-regulated brewing system holds the natural carbonation and includes an auxiliary CO2 carbonation system, allowing you to have beer "on tap", just how you like it in public.

The carbonation system lets you control the pressure used for dispensing your beer will have the perfect "head" and fresh taste for up to six months. Including with The Beer Machine is the beer mix, which is mixed with water to give you 2.6 gallons of great tasting beer. You'll also get pub-style handles, which you can personalize. The Beer Machine is compact in size so it won't take up much room on your refrigerator shelf. This is probably one of the simplest beer-making kits you'll find and great for a starter kit.

Other more extensive beer making kits are also available. Homebrewers Outpost makes quite a few different home brew kits. For under $100, you can get a complete beer making starter kit that includes all the basic brewing equipment you'll need.

With this kit, you can make 5 gallons of any type of beer you chose. Step-by-step directions and recipes come with this kit along with many of the supplies including fermenting bucket, bottling bucket with spigot, hydrometer, thermometer, bottle capper, bottle caps, sanitizer, siphon unit and more. The only thing this kit doesn't include is the bottles and a large kettle.

If you want to really expand your beer making equipment inventory, you can purchase beer making starter kits that have other accessories like a wort chiller, deluxe bottling package, secondary fermenter, deluxe kegging package and extra beer-making ingredients.

The kegging package works great for those that don't want the fuss and mess of bottling all their beer in individual bottles. This way, you'll always have beer on tap, just the way you enjoy it most.

These are just a couple of kits available. There are many more available on the market. Take your time, look around, and don't be afraid to ask questions. Beer making kits are great because they give you all the necessities you'll need to get started, along with directions.

It's like a person with no baking experience trying to decide to buy a complete cake mix or bake a cake from scratch from a recipe in their cookbook. Both are relatively easy, but the cake mix is going to be much quicker, easier and make less of a mess.

Beer making kits can be purchased relatively cheaply. The only thing some people complained about was that they eventually wanted to expand their inventory later and that made their kits unusable for them. If you're not going to be making a lot of beer, the kits may be your best option. However, if you want to make beer regularly, you're better investing in the individual supplies. From reading the list of things you'll need, you may find that you already have a lot of them in your home or shop already, thus saving you money.

USING THE INTERNET FOR HELP

You'll be amazed at the many web pages and beer making forums you'll find online. You may consider purchasing used beer making equipment. You can find some great buys on good used equipment that people no longer want. You definitely want to check out some of these places before you make any large purchases. Why pay full price on new equipment when you can get good used equipment for a fraction of the cost?

Beer making forums are a great place to discuss your beer making with others that enjoy the same hobby. You can exchange tips and learn new ideas, while searching for some of the equipment you may need. You'll also find some great new recipes from the many members here. If you have a home brew supply store in your area, they will carry new equipment, but they may also have some excellent used equipment for a good price. This is also a good place to get help or advice on anything you're not sure about. Whether you decide on purchasing the equipment little by little, all at once or going with a kit, take your time and look for the best equipment for what you need.

9
PROCESS OF HOME BREWING

Now that you've learned everything you need to learn about home brewing beer, you're all ready to start. Home brewing consists of 5 steps:

- ✓ Brewing the beer
- ✓ Cooling and Fermenting
- ✓ Priming and Bottling
- ✓ Aging
- ✓ Drinking

These directions are for 5 gallons of home brewed beer as well as basic home brewing. You may need to make some slight changes in the process depending on the equipment you're using such as a kit or the type of beer you're making.

AND FINALLY...GET BREWING!

The first thing you want to do is sterilize everything. Not just wash, but also sterilize. Bacteria may not be seen, but it can still be there and ruin your entire batch of beer. Home brew supply stores sell sanitizers or you can use bleach. Make a mix of 5 gallons of cold water per 2 ounces of *unscented* bleach, using your sink or a large tub.

Sanitize your carboy first (if you have one), followed by the other equipment. The things that fit in your sink can soak for 10 minutes, and then rinse them thoroughly.

PREPARING THE WORT

Put in approximately 1 1/2 gallons of cold water into your large brewing kettle. If the recipe you're using uses specialty grains, put them in a sparge bag and allow them to soak in the kettle and turn on the burner. When it reaches the point where it is almost going to boil, take out the sparge bag.

Add the malt extract into the kettle and bring it to a boil again. Let it boil for 20 minutes, making sure it doesn't boil over. Make sure you stir the mixture immediately and consistently so the malt doesn't stick to the bottom of the pan and burn.

ADDING THE HOPS

Put the required amount of bittering hops in a sparge back and steep for at least 30 minutes. Do not remove it before 30 minutes, as it needs this much time for all the oils to extract from the hops. If your beer recipe asks for finishing hops (which are optional), put them in another sparge bag and steep for 1 to 10 minutes. If you're after aroma, only about 2 minutes, but if it's flavor you're concerned with, then 10 minutes. Turn the heat off, take the wort off the hot burner and put the cover on the brewing pot.

CHILL THE WORT

If you have a fermenter (glass carboy), fill it half-full with cold water. If you have a wort chiller, you can use this to chill the wort. If not, fill up a bath of ice-cold water (water with ice) to sit the brewing pot in so it can chill. You may need to drain the ice water and refill with ice. If you don't have a wort chiller, you'll wish you did!

PREPARING (PROOFING) THE YEAST

While your wort is cooling down, you can prepare the yeast. Get a sterilized measuring cup and add 6 ounces of lukewarm water from the tap. Add the dried yeast to this, cover and set aside for a bit. The warm water helps to activate the yeast.

THE FERMENTER

If the brewing pot with the wort has cooled to where you can almost touch it, use a large funnel to move the wort to the glass carboy (fermenter). You may use a small **sterilized** pot instead of a funnel. Fill the fermenter with cold water until you have 5 gallons (there should be a 5-gallon mark). For the yeast to work properly, it needs oxygen, which is removed from the boiling.

To rejuvenate it with oxygen, splash the water when you're pouring it in and shake the fermenter occasionally. Pay attention to the temperature, which should be below 75 degrees Fahrenheit. Do **NOT** put the yeast in the wort until the temperature is below 75 degrees or it may die. You may want to take a reading with your hydrometer at this time to check the specific gravity.

ATTACH TUBING

Set the fermenter some place where it will stay cool, stable and out of direct sunlight. Get a large sturdy container and fill it half full with water. Put it next to the fermenter. Get sterilized tubing with outside diameter of 1 ½". Put one end in the fermenter and the other end in the container of water, making an airtight seal. This becomes a blow off tube, which will allow any excess foam to escape while the initial fermentation is taking place.

The first couple of days, you'll really see the yeast go to work as excess foam will come out the top along with air bubbling out from the container.

Some people really love watching this process, knowing their beer is being made. The tube must stay under the water to keep the seal airtight. You can remove the blow-off tube after 3 days and put in the sterilized stopper and air lock. Make sure you add about ¾" of water to the air lock or it won't work. You'll know the air lock is in place securely and has a good seal if your mixture starts to bubble. This is from the escape of carbon dioxide.

MORE WAITING...

After you've put in the air lock, the beer will need to ferment until the yeast is done, which usually takes from 5 to 14 days. It will be ready for bottling when the air lock is no longer bubbling. A hydrometer reading will tell you if the fermentation is complete. You're now ready to bottle!

BOTTLING STEPS

Once again, you need to sterilize everything including

- bottling bucket,
- hose,
- bottling tube,
- racking cane,
- bottles

The bottles need to be thoroughly cleaned before sterilizing them. Do not sterilize the caps. Put them in a small saucepan with enough water to cover them. Boil covered for five minutes, drain and cover them again until they're needed.

Add ¾ Cup of dextrose (priming sugar) in another pan with 16 ounces of water and boil for 5 minutes, cover and take off the stove.

TRANSFERRING BEER

Now you're going to transfer your beer from the fermenter to the bottling bucket. With the fermenter on a table, take out the airlock and put in the racking cane so it's approximately an inch above the yeast sediment. Attach the bottling tube and the plastic hoe to each other and fill the hose with water. Attach the hose filled with water to the racking cane and put aside for the moment. Put the bottling bucket right below the fermenter on the floor and pour the boiled dextrose in the bucket. Put the bottling tube to the bottom of the bucket and begin the siphoning process. Try to splash as little as possible as you transfer the beer.

BOTTLING THE BEER...FINALLY

Put the bottling bucket on the table. Take the hose from the racking cane and connect it to the spigot on the bucket. You'll have to use a racking cane and second siphon if you don't have a spigot.

Put an empty bottle on the floor under the bottling bucket. Open the spigot and put the bottling tube in the bottle, pressing down on the tube to get the beer moving. Fill the bottle right to the top. When the bottle is full, take out the tube. Beer will drop down about an inch. Do this on all bottles until they're all full.

CAPPING

You need to be on a steady surface for this, so you may want to stay on the floor. With the bottle capper and a cap, put a cap on the bottle. Pull the levers down with steady pressure, making sure the cap goes on straight. Crimp the cap and make sure the seal is good. Do this for all the bottles.

YOU'RE DONE!

All you have left to do is clean up your mess. Store your beer in a location with a cool and consistent temperature between 65 to 70 degrees. Let it set for about 2 weeks and be prepared to taste the best beer you've ever tasted!

RECIPES

Following are two popular home brew recipes that are easy to follow once you get the ingredients. They're perfect for a 5 gallon supply. You can modify them to your own personal tastes as you experiment.

BARLEY WINE

4 to 4 ½ ounces Galena, Eroica or Chinook bittering hops

10 to 12 pounds light malt extract

1-ounce of both Cascade and Willamette hops (finishing)

brewing yeast of your choice (many use Wyeast)

OKTOBERFEST

½-pound crystal malt specialty grain

6 to 7 lbs amber malt (this is an extract)

¼-lb. chocolate malt (this will be a specialty grain)

½ lb. Cara-Pils Munich malt (this is a specialty grain)

1 ½ to 2 ounces Saaz, Hallertauer or Tettnanger hops (this will be bittering hops)

½-ounce Saaz, Hallertauer or Tettnanger hops (this is the finishing hops)

Wyeast or brewing yeast of your choice

Some of these products may seem unfamiliar to you, but your home brew supply store should carry all of them and more. The recipes are very simple and will make a variety of different tasting beer. Once you get seriously into the home brewing of beer and other drinks, you'll find there are many recipes to be found. There's nothing more interesting than experimenting with different products for a unique taste. Your local library will have many informative books on home brewing as well as easy-to-follow recipes. The internet is also a wealth of information with their many articles and beer brewing forums.

There's nothing better when you take up a new hobby than being able to share your hobby with others that have the same enthusiasm. You can discuss recipes you've each tried, exchange helpful hints on money and time-saving techniques you may have learned. If you're considering entering amateur home brewing competitions, they'll be more fun if you know some of the participants.

10
THE FINISHED PRODUCT

Once you've finished making your beer, all you have to do is wait out the correct amount of time until you can finally taste it. Although every beer maker swears their home brew is the best they've ever tasted, it may seem strange to you at the first sampling. After all, you've been drinking commercially brewed beer for years and this is a change. Once you've had a few of your beers, you'll never want to go back to store-bought beer again.

When you pour your first beer into a glass, you'll find a little sediment on the bottom of the bottle. You won't want to drink this, although it won't hurt you. Your fresh beer will have a great taste when you open your first bottle. Your beer can be stored in your fridge for a long time; although it might not last all that long once everyone gets a taste.

The most fun part of brewing your own beer is experimenting with different ingredients to increase the alcohol content or give it an extra pizzazz. For instance, many people make a home brewed beer with maple syrup and swear it's the best they've ever made. Once you have mastered making the perfect tasting beer, you may want to experiment with wine making, which is just as much fun.

HOME BREW FAQ

- **Most recipes say home brewing takes a couple of weeks. Does it have to take this long?**
  While you may find some recipes that take slightly less time, most home brew needs this time to properly ferment and age. It's more than worth the wait.

- **Do I really need all the equipment they say I have to have?**
  You won't need every little item, although many of them are for your convenience. However, some of the items you already have in your kitchen or garage may work just fine.

- **Is sterilization really necessary?**
  Absolutely! Not only can bacteria in your beer cause an entire batch to have to be thrown out, but it can also make you sick.

- **Is home brewing safe?**
  Home brewing is perfectly safe as well as being fun! The only time you may have a problem is if bacteria finds its way into your beer. Proper sterilization will eliminate this problem.

- **Some of my bottles exploded. Did I do something wrong or were the bottles bad?**
  When bottles explode, they were filled too high or there was too much dextrose (sugar) put in your beer. The bottles should be filled only halfway up the neck. If you did not wait the required time before bottling the beer, the sugar may not have had time to break down the alcohol, which may cause them to explode.

- **Why does my beer have a bitter taste?**
  Everyone has different taste buds, but you may try to put less hops in your beer next time you make it.

- **Should I use malt extract or specialty grains when I make my beer?**
  Using grains is a little more complicated than using malt extracts. Malt extract is a powder or syrup that's made from grains. If you're a beginner at making your own beer, you're better off staying with malt extract until you really get the hang of experimenting with home brewing. Some of the best beers in the world are made with malt extract.

- **This is my first time making my own beer. I've read everything I can to learn the process. I want to try making beer, but I don't want to spend a lot of money just starting out. Should I buy all the required equipment or just buy the kit?**
  Although having all the required equipment will be convenient for you in the future, all the items may seem overwhelming for the first time home brewer. You may want to purchase the kit for your first beer making adventure. The advantage of using a home brew kit is that there are fewer items to worry about, you have everything you need and there are easy to follow directions. What many enjoy about the kits are that the recipes they include are based on their kits, so you don't have to alter any directions.

- **How do I know the best place to buy my supplies and equipment?**
  Once you have made your first batch of beer, you'll know a little more about what it entails and what you need. Shop around in your local area as well as online. The best way to get the best equipment for your money is to research what you need and find the best price.